BORN
for the
JOB

BORN
for the
JOB

A Collection of
Amusingly Apt Names

James Steen
and
Dominic Midgley

Michael O'Mara Humour

First published in Great Britain in 2004 by
Michael O'Mara Books Limited
9 Lion Yard
Tremadoc Road
London SW4 7NQ

A CIP catalogue record for this book is available from the
British Library

ISBN 1-84317-099-X

1 3 5 7 9 10 8 6 4 2

Designed and typeset by Design 23

Printed and bound in England by Cox & Wyman Ltd,
Reading, Berks

CONTENTS

INTRODUCTION 7

ALL CREATURES GREAT AND SMALL 9

UP THE HIGH STREET 13

BRICKIES, CHIPPIES AND CHUMS 17

LAW AND ORDER 23

DOCTORS AND NURSES 27

IN THE DENTIST'S CHAIR 39

MONEY MAKES THE WORLD GO ROUND 43

A FISHY BUSINESS 47

FOOD AND DRINK 51

GOOD SPORTS 57

MEN (AND WOMEN) OF THE CLOTH 61

LEGAL EAGLES 67

IN GOVERNMENT CIRCLES 73

LET'S FACE THE MUSIC 77

DOWN ON THE FARM 81

IN THE PRESS OFFICE 85

IN MEDIA CIRCLES 89

ON THE ROAD 93

EDUCATION, EDUCATION, EDUCATION 97

TV LAND 101

WATERWORKS 105

THE FINAL CURTAIN 109

IN A LEAGUE OF THEIR OWN –
A MISCELLANY 113

INTRODUCTION

On 13 May 2002, we ran the following short item in 'The Scurra', the column we write for the *Daily Mirror*: 'The press officer at Playtex, makers of Wonderbra, is called Kate Bosomworth.' We had already featured a couple of mentions of people whose names uncannily matched their jobs, including Alan Cheesman, the cheese-and-wine party organizer, and Simon Burns, the MP who was worried about the effects of sunburn on the British electorate. Yet it was the mention of Ms Bosomworth that really caught the imagination of Scurra readers, and in the weeks and months that followed, nominations flooded in on a daily basis. Each one we published prompted another spate of contributions, of which this compilation is the result.

There is nothing profound about the attraction of this occasional feature. Quite simply, each suggestion brought an immediate smile to our faces, whether it was Dorcas Binns, the woman in charge of rubbish collection at Stroud District Council, the speed cop called Tim Brake, or even

Mark Passmore . . . the driving instructor.

The potency of their appeal lies in the fact that all are the names of real people in real jobs. In time, we amassed hundreds of examples and the best of them are collected together in this little book. If you would like to help in the collection of hundreds more, please email us at bornforthejob@hotmail.com.

James Steen and Dominic Midgley
April 2004

ALL CREATURES GREAT AND SMALL

Pieter Kat

Lion researcher

Carolyn and Tom Screech

Owl sanctuary proprietors

Pat Sparrowhawk

BIRD PHOTOGRAPHER

There's a wonderful owl sanctuary at Goss Moor,
St Columb, Cornwall, which is run by a couple
called Carolyn and Tom Screech. They've called it
The Screech Owl Sanctuary.

Gill Sabotig

I would like to nominate Pieter Kat, a lion
researcher in Africa.

V. Cain Lydiate

I met a gentleman recently who works for the Rural Payments Agency at Exeter. His name was Mr Squirrel, and he had come to our farm to inspect our tree plantation.

Gill Sabotig

The spokeswoman for the Berlin Animal House, an animal welfare group that looks after German cats and dogs, is called Carola Ruff.

Ruki Sayid

One of the contacts at the East Anglia branch of the Royal Society for the Protection of Birds (RSPB) is a Miss Stork.

Sarah Hapuarachchi

Printed in the *Henley Standard*, on 14 June 2002, alongside a photograph of a bird, an article described how a cheeky red kite flew down from the sky, spied some food and took off again with a piece of bacon in its beak. The man responsible for supplying the newspaper with dramatic pictures of the bird swooping into his back garden was an amateur cameraman by the name of Pat Sparrowhawk.

P. J. Hickey

In the 1970s, when I was studying psychology and zoology, the world's most respected ethologists (researchers in the behaviour of animals from aardvarks to zebras) included one chap called Lionel Tiger and another named Robin Fox.

Geoff Nicholls

We used to have a vet at the Holsworthy surgery called Mr Death.

Gill Sabotig

I recently discovered that the editor of the Guide Dogs for the Blind charity magazine is called Tracey Gurr, as in 'woof, woof, grrrrr'.

Rachel Pavitt

UP THE HIGH STREET

Reid & Wright
Newsagent and stationer

H. Clogg and Son
Orthopaedic footwear

I. Blewitt
Bookmaker

In 1940 I worked in a butcher's shop owned by a man who was very adept at removing meat from the bone. Perhaps that's why he was called Mr Bone.

C. Highams

There is a librarian at Consett library called Les Storey.

John Heslop

My sister-in-law's maiden name was Carcas, and although this doesn't qualify *her* as someone who was born for the job, her father was in fact a butcher in Lewisham, South London.

Mrs E. Hutchinson

There's a butcher's shop in Dartmouth which is called Cutmores (the real family name of the shopkeeper who earns his living cutting up meat all day long).

Stella Hender

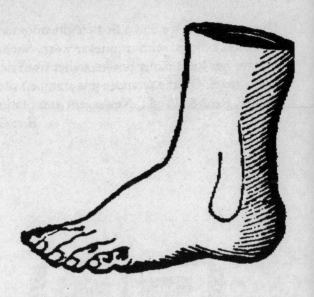

In the Mile End Road, East London, there is an H. Clogg and Son, Orthopaedic Footwear.

Peter Aldridge

My dad used to let a shop in Dartmouth, Devon, to a bookmaker called I. Blewitt.

Tim Perring

As a child I enjoyed a holiday in Mousehole, Cornwall, where I recall there was a butcher named Kneebone.

John Heslop

During the war we had a Scotch girl from near Inverness billeted with us on war work. She used to have her local paper posted to her from her home town. On the wrapper was stamped the sender, Reid & Wright, Newsagent and Stationer.

Bert Choney

BRICKIES, CHIPPIES AND CHUMS

Fiddler and Leake
Roofing contractors

Wackett Brothers
Demolition contractors

Alan Joiner
Woodwork specialist

I remember seeing in Weymouth, Dorset, a building business that was (unfortunately, some might think) named after the family that ran it . . . Crumbleholme.

Bert Smith

I have just discovered S. A. Woodsmith, who just happens to be a joinery and building contractor in Leeds.

Ann E. Milner

When I lived in Herne Bay, I knew a woodworker called Alan Joiner.

Frances Harben

Mr Charlie Shivers –
Heating Supplies –
Toombridge, N. Ireland.
Michael Rooney

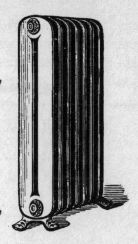

Some years ago we had
some building work done
and the plumber's name
was Arthur Freshwater.
Bert Choney

In Market Harborough, Leicestershire, there's a
plasterer called Dave Smooth ('overskimming old
plaster a speciality').

Mrs I. P. Webb

This weekend I had a bit of a flood in my kitchen due to using the hosepipe on the taps. Today I rang Blackpool council to ask if I could have an outdoor tap fitted. I was told it should not be a problem, provided that I first write for permission from . . . Mr Fawcett.

Terry Bennett

When I lived in Ilford, Essex, during the 1960s and 1970s we regularly received leaflets from a firm of roofers called Fiddler and Leake.

Henry Thomas

We have a local plumber called Dave Tapp.

Dr J. R. Cook

My nephew and son, Richard and Barry Plank are
both scaffolders working in the Brighton area.

Barry Plank

We have a building merchant who is called Mr
Underwood.

Mrs F. Thompson

My chum, Donald Attwood is a carpenter by
trade, so frequently he's 'with' wood if not actually
'at' it.

R. Wallace Robertson

How about a Newbury customer I met recently
called Mr Digger. His job? Head gardener.

Stan Harper

For the last ten years I've been working with an electrician called Jack Sparks.

Janet Hodge

There was a firm of Demolition Contractors in Romford, Essex, called Wackett Brothers.

William Golding

I used a carpenter in Selsey, West Sussex, who was called Craig Allwood.

Terry Hall

LAW
AND
ORDER

Des Lawless
Police Spokesman

Officer
Paul Officer
Royal Protection Officer

Inspector Bollard
Northampton Traffic Division

When I was in the Birmingham city police during the 1950s and 1960s, the man who was in charge of communications and repairs was a certain Mr Morse.

Pat Shearon

An article in my local newspaper (*Luton on Sunday*) mentioned a police spokesman whose name is Des Lawless.

Alf Burgess

Constable Constable worked at Bakewell police station when I was in CID. And when I was a uniform sergeant at Chesterfield police station I was lucky enough to work on the same shift as Sergeant Sergeant.

Name withheld

We had a police chief inspector called Grabham.

Ken Eggleton

The Blackpool police officer who was sent to deal with the problem yobs in Rhodes is Chief Superintendent Andy Rhodes.

Terry Bennett

In February 2004 the *Liverpool Echo* featured an article about how 'Two corrupt Inland Revenue workers who swindled £250,000 of taxpayers' money were today jailed for four years. John Fidler and Marie Till recruited nine people to instigate their fraud.' Talk about fiddling the till.

Kevin Price, Keith Wilson and Stuart Ogilvie

The man who is the liaison officer between Lancashire Police and Blackpool Football Club is a certain Sergeant Lawman.

Chris Hewitt

There was an inspector in Belfast called Nick Purse.

Brian Fisher

On 22 May 2002, Surrey police announced that the copper who nabbed forty speeding motorists in Woking is PC Tim Brake.

David Crawley

The royal protection officer who was always to be found at Prince Charles's side was one Paul Officer. In other words, Officer Officer.

C. Hutchins

During the 1980s, the police inspector in charge of the traffic division in Northampton was Inspector Bollard. His responsibilities presumably included overseeing the use, positioning and removal of road bollards etc.

Pete Smith

DOCTORS
AND
NURSES

Dr Wellbaby

Paediatrician

**Nurse
Stephanie Gore**

Burns and plastics unit

Dr Payne
General
Practitioner

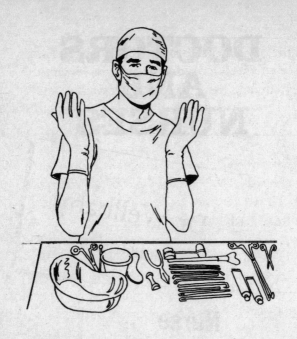

The Chief Executive of Heywood & Middleton Primary Care Trust is Keith Surgeon.

Ele Collington

The best name I ever came across was that of a paediatrician who was once employed at the hospital where I now work. His name? Dr Wellbaby.

Tony Pressley

In the day ward at Broadgreen Hospital, I was once very well looked after by a nurse with the very suitable name of Alison Bedward.

Bernard Eaton

When my girlfriend was pregnant I took her to the local hospital to see the gynaecologist. His name was Dr Watson; my girlfriend's name is Miss Holmes. Elementary.

Stephen Maxwell Duerden

My grandma was a nurse who eventually became a 'Sister'. Her maiden name was Ward.

Paul Ballard

In the 1950s, in Dawbers sanatorium in Lincoln, there were two brothers who worked there as nurses whose surname was Pain.

Arthur Bilton

There's a lady practising in chiropody in Upper Tean, Staffordshire. Her name is Joanne Foot.

Pete Braime

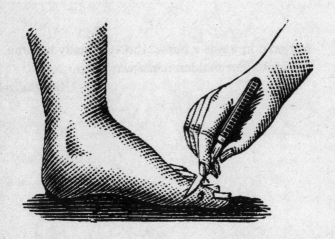

My friend Chris used to go to a physiotherapist called Katherine Bendall, who certainly made him bend all the parts that needed to get better.

Mansell Scott Sissons

I've just received a press invite to a seminar for the Family Heart Association conducted by Dr John Reckless.

Name withheld

While working at a large general hospital in London in the 1960s, one of the physiotherapists who worked in orthopaedics was a Swedish girl called Armbuster.

Joe Monro

A Nobel Prize-winning scientist will feature in a BBC programme called *Magic Bullets* which focuses on his work in the treatment of cancer. His name . . . Paul Nurse.

Steve Purcell and Eric Gower

My mother's GP in Stanley, County Durham, is called Dr Hijab (as in jab – injection).

Miss I. Murphy

It just so happens that the head of Accident & Emergency at Leicester Royal Infirmary is Mr Bodiwala.

Kash Patel

In the late 1960s, I worked in a large psychiatric hospital in the north of England. Brian Porter was a porter, Steven Cook was a cook, Denzil Nurse was a nurse, and there was a patient called D. Nutter.

Bernie Fish

A friend went to the doctors about a heart operation and saw his GP – Dr Coffin.

S. Vaughan

During a court case in the USA in the 1980s, a doctor was prosecuted for using his own semen in artificial insemination and claiming that that the donors were in fact university professors and doctors. His lawyer's name was Randy Bellows.

Chris Roper

When I was in hospital recently the male nurse whose duties included administering enemas was called Robert Sole. He wasn't allowed to shorten Robert to R. when filling in his reports.

Dave Harvey

My Consultant Opthalmic Anaesthetist who works at Moorfields Eye Hospital is called Dr Christine Moore. Hence Dr C. Moore.

Mr Richard Ismail, Registered Operating
Department Practitioner Locum

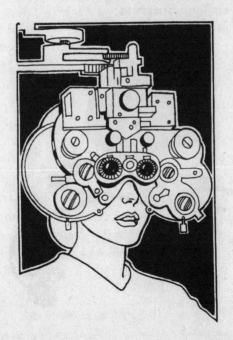

When I was in South Africa my gynaecologist was called Dr Crutchfield.

Wendy Barnard

I recently visited a relative on a Burns and Plastics ward and she told me she was being seen by a nurse called Stephanie Gore.

Andrew Quirke

Compass magazine recently featured a photograph of one Dr John Sneezum.

John Brookes

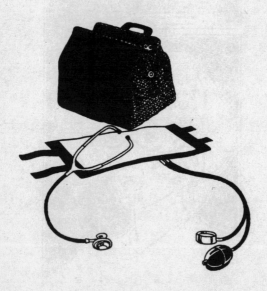

While in South Africa, my husband had to visit an urologist. His name was Dr P. Allwright!

Wendy Barnard

I attend a diabetes clinic at Burnley General Hospital and was recently sent for a blood test. I was most surprised to find that the new doctor who had asked for the blood test was called Dr Sugar. Ironic or what?

Barry Miller

While awaiting the results of a mammogram at Stoke Mandeville hospital some years ago, I was reading a card taped to the wall when I noticed that the name of the admin person was Mr Titley.

Kaye Brister

We have a Dr A. P. U. King in our group practice.

Name withheld

Our local surgery has a nice young GP called Dr Payne.

Norma Miles

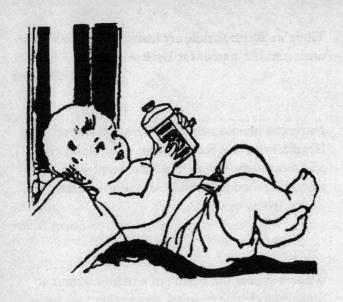

The surgeon who delivered my son by Caesarean was called Mr Cutter.

Mrs A. V. Vincent

While inspecting fishing nets on the Helford River in Cornwall, a friend of mine was called to the assistance of a family who were stranded on a mudbank in their small boat. After a tricky rescue, he was thanked by the 'captain' of the vessel, an anaesthetist by the name of Dr Sleep.

Mike Farr

There's a doctor in the area who suffers the unfortunate name of Dr Useless.

Tony Richards

According to a letter in *Front* magazine (July 2002) the name of the consultant at West Middlesex Hospital's day surgery unit who performs vasectomies is called . . . Mr Bellringer.

Ken Andrew

A couple of years ago I had a problem with my waterworks but it was ably sorted out by the consultant, Mr Dick.

Graham Snow

In Felixstowe we have the jolliest doctor called Dr Feltwell.

Sarah Gillespie

Some fifteen years ago I had a mastectomy. The surgeon who performed the operation was a Mr Boobis.

Hazel Brewin

The BBC produced a television series called *Obsessions* recently, which featured a scientist who is pioneering a deep brain stimulation technique to cure obsessive compulsives. His name? Professor Nuttin of the University of Leuvin, Belgium!

Steve Purcell

Several years ago I had to attend a clinic at the local hospital for people with leg ulcers and various other leg problems. Appropriately enough, the consultant's name was Mr Standeven.

Hazel Knight

IN THE DENTIST'S CHAIR

Peter Savage

'The Dentist with Gentle Hands'

Valerie Chew

DENTAL HYGIENIST

 Major
Screech

Dentist

We have an excellent dentist
in Weston-Super-Mare
whose name is Mrs Tingle.
Brian Carrett

Many years ago when we lived in London, we had
a dentist whose name was Mr Phang.

Sue Elliott

There's a dentist in Belfast called – Peter Savage.
His company logo is 'The Dentist with Gentle
Hands' which should reassure potential patients
who would otherwise be discouraged by his name.
Anna Heath

There was a dentist
in Leeds in the late
1940s whose
surname was
Pullem.
Pam Cory

From 1961 to 1962, I used to cycle from my family home in Boreham Wood, Hertfordshire, to see my girlfriend who lived in New Barnet. On the return journey I would chuckle as I cycled past a dental surgery bearing a large nameplate in Station Road. The dentist's name was Dr Carole Sreek.

Name withheld

Many years ago I was a patient of a dentists' practice in Sheffield. The names on the door were Killem & Dearden.

Judith McFarlane

There was a dentist in Minehead called Major Screech, who had a practice in the town just after the war.

Mike Heard

In the 1980s Lever Bros Warrington appointed a dental hygienist / advisor. Her name was Valerie Chew.

Terry Watt

My dentist in Doncaster is called Mr Payne.

Brian Fisher

This triumvirate of dentists have just written to me asking me to pay up: David J. Pullen, Charles Killick and Bethan Bloodworth.

Mrs C. Russell

My old dentist in Worcester Park, Surrey, who I believe still practises his skills, is called De Groot (pronounced 'dig root'). How very apt.

Pete Baker

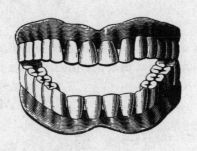

MONEY MAKES THE WORLD GO ROUND

A. FIDDLEMAN
ACCOUNTANT

R. L. PROFFITT
HSBC Bank plc

Wayne Banks
BARCLAYS BANK

Recently I received a letter from HSBC Bank plc in Sheffield that was signed by a Mr R. L. Proffitt.

Ken Horton

We have a firm of chartered accountants and taxation advisers in Uckfield called Swindells and Gentry.

D. Hollands and Chris Lassman

Say 'ello, 'ello, 'ello to the cop who works for Metropolitan Police's Cheque and Credit Card Fraud Squad. His name? Detective Sergeant Richard Money.

Name withheld

I worked for a firm in south-west London where there was an accountant called Mr A. Fiddleman.

Carol Jones

While serving my apprenticeship with T. Partingtons in Oldham, the wages manager was called Stan Cheetham.

Neil Robinson

In the Torquay branch of Barclays Bank I was
served by Wayne Banks.

Mrs Christine Hopcott

There is a Kenyan treasury official called Mr
Koinage.

Jimmy Stevens

About fifteen years ago, I was on Schedule 'D' for
income tax – which meant yearly accounts. I was
amused to find that the person dealing with my
claim at the Birkenhead Tax Office was one Mr
Robin Bastard.

Max Cowell

The treasurer of the Crowthorne Village Singers proves to be suitably named for her job. She is called Margaret Greedy.

P. Hickey

I recently received correspondence from a representative of Homeowners Friendly Society of Harrogate, who advised me that the savings plan I have been paying into for the last ten years is now worth 20 per cent less than I have paid in, due to a 'considerable downward trend in the stock market'. His name was Steve Treasure.

J. Eyton-Jones

What about the managing director of Lloyds Bank Securities Services who's called Wayne Kitcat? Borrowing the chocolate bar's slogan, he's ideally named to take a break-in. Or is that stretching it? *(It's stretching it – Ed.)*

J. O'Neil

A FISHY BUSINESS

Ada Chipp

Smith's Fish and Chip shop

Franz Fischler

European Fisheries Commissioner

Joanne Trout

Newquay Aquarium Centre
Spokeswoman

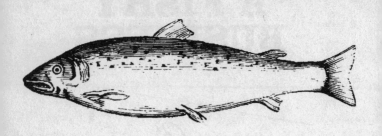

How about my name? Years ago I was managing
director of a company that manufactured fish-
frying equipment.

Terry Haddock

For a number of years my mother-in-law worked
behind the counter of Smith's Fish and Chip shop
in Epping High Road. Her name? Mrs Ada Chipp.

John Ross

In Redcar there was a family of Picknetts. Many of
them were fishermen.

M. H.

In January 2004 *The Scotsman* reported that 'the European Fisheries Commissioner was facing unprecedented pressure to make sweeping changes to the new North Sea fisheries regime', which were due to come into force. And who exactly is the European Fisheries Commissioner? He's none other than Franz Fischler.

Dave Ellis

While on holiday in the West Country recently, I was watching the local news when an item came on about the Newquay Aquarium Centre. The spokeswoman who was being interviewed was called Joanne Trout.

Alison Dillingham

The Applecross Inn in Wester Ross, the Highlands, is the reigning UK Fish Pub of the Year. And who is the owner of this magnificent restaurant? None other than Judith Fish.

Name withheld

FOOD AND DRINK

MR AND MRS LES BREWIN

Cross Foxes
Public House

PROFESSOR MIKE LEAN

Nutrition Expert

Andy Vine

Oddbins' Wine Buyer

The chief executive of the Food Standards Agency is Geoffrey Podger (as in podgy).

Will Jenkins

The wine buyer at Oddbins is Andy Vine.

Name withheld

I worked at Tesco in Bishops Cleeve, Gloucestershire, a few years ago, where the woman in charge of bread and cakes was Collette Cakebread.

David Kelley

The beer buyer for Somerfield supermarkets is known as Andy Carling.

Edna Neaves

The person in charge of catering for the Commonwealth Games in Manchester, who also did catering for the Sydney Olympics, was called A. Sweetapple.

Sally Leitch-Devlin and Tom Gordon

The South West Sales rep for Smiles Beer is Tony Vile.

Stella Hender

What about the nutrition expert whose name is Professor Mike Lean?

Julian Corlett

Years ago the manager at the Express Dairies in Dewsbury, West Yorkshire, was Mr Buttery.

Irene Patterson

Unbelievably Claire Pickup works for the chocolate biscuit brand p... p... p... p pick up a Penguin. She is category trade manager.

Damon Statt

The former general manager of the Yates Wine Lodge pub by Blackpool North Pier is none other than Mr Ken Barwise.

Ian Turner

In the *Daily Mirror* an article once referred to a chef whose name just happened to be Jacqui Kitchen.

Alf Burgess

The first job I had was in the 1950s when I worked in a pie shop. The manageress was a Miss Pye.

Pat Thomas

Some years ago, there was a greengrocer in Nottingham called Mr Onion.

Nadine Walters

The chap who organizes cheese and wine parties for Sainsbury's is called . . . Alan Cheesman.

J. Grove

How about the long-established milking machine manufacturers in Salisbury . . . John Wallis Titt.

Steve Oxbrow

The drinks club manager for Sainsbury's is a certain Brandy Renton.

Pauline Nicholl

I recently saw a local milk delivery vehicle belonging to a firm called Hael and Son, that bore the slogan: 'We deliver through rain sleet snow, Hael and Son.'

Paul Cross

The company doctor at the Guinness brewery, Park Royal, London, was the competitively named Dr Watney.

Michael Linnane

The landlord and landlady of the Cross Foxes public house in Prestatyn are Mr and Mrs Les Brewin.

Harold Martin

GOOD SPORTS

Buster Footman

Football Club Physiotherapist

Wolfgang Wolf

Wolfsburg FC Coach

Peter Bowler

SOMERSET COUNTY CRICKET CLUB

For many years, principally in the days before darts became a major television sport, the world's top darts tournament was run and sponsored by the *News of the World*. The man who for many of those years acted as the MC was called Les Treble.

Roy Stockdill

There's a veteran county cricketer called Peter Bowler who plays for Somerset. According to his career statistics he was probably more successful as a batter than a bowler, but nevertheless, he's got a great name for a cricketer.

Fiona Byrne

I was at the Newbury Show yesterday and was delighted to see that the Falconry Flying Display was being given by 'Jim Chick and his bird'.

Mandy Southwick

Wolfsburg FC are coached by Wolfgang Wolf.

Richard Elton

The race director for the Bristol half-marathon is one Ms de Hoof.

Gren Tapp

If ever there was a rugby player born for the job it has to be the sportsman who plays centre for the French national rugby union side. His name is Damien Traille (pronounced Try).

Fiona Byrne

One member of the brilliant cheerleading squad that roots for the Taranaki Rugby football union is called Wendy Topless.

Name withheld

AFC Wimbledon have a midfield player called Lee Passmore. Just for the record, AFC Wimbledon do try to play a passing game so I guess the name is appropriate.

Dave Kemp

The man who has investigated the power of Mike Tyson's punches at Loughborough University is Michael Pain.

Barry May

The owner of Top Gear Karting in the city of Durham is Tom Tyreman.

Contributed, appropriately enough, by Rachel Carhart

My friend is a belly-dancing teacher. Her name is Carol A. Button (as in belly).

Treza Hammond

There's a Cameroonian footballer called Joseph-Desire Job (although I don't know if he's bad enough for his name to suit his job).

Sally Smith

I was recently reminded that Southend United's old physio was the aptly named Buster Footman. We were never quite sure if that was a nickname or not.

Richard Bradford

MEN (AND WOMEN) OF THE CLOTH

Reverend
Alison Christian
ST JOHN'S CHURCH

Reverend
Larry Goodpaster

CHRISTIAN PREACHER

REVEREND
Ian Bishop
Middlewich St Michael and
All Angels Church

We had a vicar at Madron who was called Reverend Toogood.

Terri Strick

In my church magazine it mentions a visiting American preacher named Reverend Larry Goodpaster.

Ted Harrison

The Prebendary of St Patrick's Cathedral, Northern Ireland, is the Reverend Dr Bert Tosh.

Jenni Jones

There is one Reverend Alison Christian who is the vicar or rector of St John's Church in Stanmore, Middlesex.

Robert Hailes

The vicar who married us was named Reverend H. Massiah. His blessings must have been sincere as we are into our 59th year of happiness together.

Amelia Salmon

When I was married at Bolton Percy church, the curate was the Reverend Lord.

Isabel Walker

How about the Reverend Ian Bishop from
Middlewich St Michael and All Angels Church?

Nicola Irwin

Many years ago, while working in Germany, I met
an army padre who was called J. C. Cross.

Graham Wright

In the 1970s in Stalbridge, Dorset, the board
outside the church would read: 'Morning Service
– The Reverend Joseph Heaven. Evening Service –
The Reverend Pugh'.

John Ryan

What about our local vicar, whose name is Father
Brian Godsell?

J. Kennedy

I remember a Cardinal Syn of the Philippines a few years ago. The rumour was that when an Irish priest was found to have a grown-up son, he fled there and began his confession, 'Forgive me, Syn, for I have fathered . . .'

R. Musgrove

The manager of Easton Christian Family Centre in Bristol is called Mike Badman.

Stella Hender

LEGAL EAGLES

THE RIGHT HONOURABLE
SIR IGOR JUDGE
LORD JUSTICE OF APPEAL

FRANCES CROOK
Howard League for
Penal Reform
Spokesperson

Wright, Hassall & Co.
SOLICITORS

There's a chap called The Right Honourable Sir Igor Judge who is a Lord Justice of Appeal, so he's also known as Judge Judge.

Steve Armstrong

We are moving into a new office on Piccadilly in London, and while looking at the list of other tenants in the building, we came across a company called Bull and Bull Solicitors.

Claire Otway

The regional director of the Legal Services Commission – the man who decides who gets what in terms of Legal Aid – is called Andy Grant.

Mark Hanley

The spokesperson for the Howard League for Penal Reform is Frances Crook.

The Niceboys

There's another senior appeal court judge called Sir John Laws (Lord Justice Laws).

Matt

I recently heard about a female solicitor with the unlikely – but completely genuine – name of Sue Wright.

Maria Mawson

When I went to a firm of solicitors in Loughborough, Leicestershire, to have a will made, I was impressed to discover that the particular man who prepared the will for me was a Michael Wills.

Norma Ridket

In Leamington Spa, Warwickshire, there is a firm of solicitors called Wright, Hassall & Co.

Sally Southall

In March 2004 the *Richmond & Twickenham Times* printed an item regarding the appointment of new magistrates to the Richmond Magistrates Court, one of whom was a Dr Ann Prison.

Gerry Hollands

My mother's divorce lawyer in Farnham, Surrey, was a Mr Loveless.

Gail Pocknell

There was once a firm of solicitors in Sligo, Eire, called Argue and Phibbs.

Don O'Connor and Maurice Henry

'Boy George agreed to pay £100,000 libel damages after he allegedly claimed that a man he punched in a nightclub was to blame,' reported the *Evening Mail* on 26 February 2004. 'A judge in London's High Court heard that in June 2002, Andrew Thompson was working at the Sweet Suite nightclub in London's Soho when he was punched by Boy George.'

The article continued: 'Mr Thompson's solicitor said five months later Boy George gave an interview to a magazine in which he alleged that Mr Thompson had insulted him. Mr Thompson had sought an apology and withdrawal of the allegations but Boy George had refused. Boy George had now agreed to apologize and pay damages of £10,000.'

And the name of Mr Thompson's solicitor? Hanna Basha.

Alice Bedford

IN GOVERNMENT CIRCLES

Judith Stones
Aberdeen City Council
Archaeological Dept.

Hilary Armstrong

Government Chief Whip

Ian Poll
Head of Democratic Services,
Newcastle Council

What about the Labour MP who is a junior minister in the department of health, who therefore spends his time thinking about the health of British men and women? He's the Member for Thanet South, Stephen Ladyman.

Stuart Pierce

The Government Chief Whip is Hilary Armstrong. When you consider that Whips have to be tough, no-nonsense sort of people, isn't her surname appropriate? Indeed, at Westminster many of us Labour backbenchers call her Strong Arm (although not to her face).

Name withheld

How about this one: Ian Poll – Head of Democratic Services, Newcastle Council.

Richard Myton

Trade Secretary Patricia Hewitt was questioned in the Commons on 24 March 2004, about water services. The MP who quizzed her? Swindon's Julia Drown.

Felix Williams

In April, 2002, one MP tabled a Parliamentary question, about 'what measures will be taken to promote the use of sun protection creams over the summer'. He was the Conservative Member for Chelmsford West . . . Simon Burns.

Name withheld

At the archaeological department at Aberdeen City Council there was a Judith Stones.

Neil Watson

The government's new House Price Index was compiled by statisticians including the appropriately named David Wall.

Clinton Manning

Seen on Google news: 'Foreign Minister
Alexander Downer has warned that Australians
face a serious threat of further terrorist attacks
despite security co-operation being stepped up in
the wake of the Bali bombings.'
Well, if you are going to tell someone bad news, it
might as well be from A. Downer.

Claire Otway

The head of Network Management in the
Highways Directorate of the National Assembly
for Wales is Mr R. Cone. He is a civil servant
responsible for trunk roads in Wales.

Ian Miller

LET'S FACE THE MUSIC

Albert Tinkler

PIANIST

Mavis Blow

Baritone horn player, Appledore Brass Band

Robert Wackett

DRUMMER

A brilliant Midlands pianist recently passed away. His name was Mr Albert Tinkler, i.e. A. Tinkler.

D. Darby

Guess who's handling publicity for the BBC's *Number One Party* celebrating fifty years of the UK pop charts? That's right, pop-pickers . . . it's Jack Tsang.

Steve Purcell

The baritone horn player of the Appledore (Brass) Band is Mavis Blow.

Ray Cooper

Seen in the Musicians' Union Members' directory
under Percussion . . . Robert Wackett, Drums.

John Morley

The General Manager of The Ambache Chamber
Orchestra is Sue Sharpe.

Maria Mawson

What about the sound engineer who works for The Smiths? He's called Grant Showbiz (although I don't know if that's his real surname).

S. Partridge

The former musical director and principal conductor of the City of Birmingham Symphony Orchestra is one Sir Simon Rattle.

Graham Williams

DOWN
ON THE
FARM

David Pigg

Farmer

PETER BULL

FARM MANAGER

Michael

Chickhen

NATIONAL FARMERS' UNION

The head of the National Farmers Union in
Wolston, Coventry, is a chap called Michael
Chickhen.

Sheena Renaldo

At the department for Environment, Food and
Rural Affairs at Kenton Bar, the person who acted
as spokeswoman during the Foot and Mouth crisis
was Rebecca Cowburn.

Nikki Bourne

Our new farm manager is called Peter Bull.

Gill Thexton

A report in the *Morning Star* lists four joint hunt masters who've been suspended for breaking the hunt rules. One of them is a farmer called Roger Dungworth.

Red Ted

As seen on *Channel 4 News*: David Pigg, farmer.

Jenny Morrison

I live in a village in Kent called Staplehurst where there is a Farmer Greengrow, who's a retired livestock farmer.

John Baker

The official of the Stroud Community Agriculture Project who is seeking names for three young Shorthorn cows is the aptly named Laurence Dungworth.

Name withheld

IN THE PRESS OFFICE

ANDREW HEAVENS

St John the Evangelist
Episcopalian Church press officer

Kate Bosomworth

Wonderbra Press Officer

Sandi Digby

PR DEPARTMENT, DIGGERLAND

In January 2004, an employee of the respected public relations firm Bell Pottinger emailed the national media with a briefing note which he suggested 'might be of interest in relation to the Government's current campaign aimed at tackling obesity'.

The briefing read: 'The catering and hospitality industry is coming under increasing pressure from the Government and consumers to adopt a more healthy policy with regard to the food served to its customers. Key issues are:

1. High salt levels in the British diet
2. Obesity amongst British children has reached an all time high and continues to rise. Early signs of heart disease and diabetes are becoming more common in children and adolescents
3. Fad diets are sending out mixed messages to consumers who are now confused about how to eat healthily

Caterers have to become more responsible about the foods that they serve, taking into account a host of health concerns affecting the industry. At Avenance, who feed over a quarter of a million workers every day, Raffaella Piovesan has taken on the role of group dietician and lifestyle expert. Her purpose is to put into practice her philosophy of promoting optimal health and well-being across all sectors. Raffaella's experience spans assessing and advising on NHS hospital menus to analysing the athletes' meals at the Commonwealth Games in 2002.

She has strong opinions on fad diets and is against the now infamous Atkins diet. Raffaella feels that celebrities should be more responsible as they are icons to our children and they could be far more actively influential in promoting a healthy diet and lifestyle. She believes that parents, schools and the Government each have a part to play in educating children on healthy eating.

If you would like to interview Raffaella to discuss the above or talk to her about any other issues affecting the food industry please call me . . .'

And who was the press officer awaiting calls about obesity and diets? Nick Cakebread.

The PR lady at Diggerland, the theme park where you can drive JCBs and bulldozers on a building site, is called Sandi Digby.

Jonathan Francis

The person who works in the marketing department of our charity WaterAid is Sharon Brand-Shelf.

Jules Acton

The press officer for St John the Evangelist Episcopalian Church in Forres is Andrew Heavens.

Neil Watson

The PR person responsible for organizing 'Santa's Kingdom', a snow-filled Christmas extravaganza held at Wembley Exhibition Centre, is called Vicki Snow.

Ruki Sayid

The press officer for Wonderbra is . . . Kate Bosomworth.

Steve Purcell

IN MEDIA CIRCLES

JEFFERSON HACK

JOURNALIST

Anita Singh

SHOWBIZ CORRESPONDENT,
PRESS ASSOCIATION

Enda Storey

Journalist

On the *PM* programme on Tuesday night there
was a piece about two bells that were stolen. The
piece was presented by a reporter called Jane Peel.

A. J. Clatworthy

Watching a BBC news programme last night, I
was amused to see their environment
correspondent doing a piece about rubbish. His
surname? Heap.

Mike Graham

We have a journalist in Ireland with the apt name – Enda Storey.

Nigel O'Gorman

In a cutting from my local newspaper, it reports: 'Thousands of people within the borough are regular cannabis smokers. These figures will only get worse, according to police struggling to catch the culprits. They say the imminent relaxation in the law will only encourage more users and lead to a downward spiral with drug-taking on the streets becoming commonplace and more children being sucked into the drug culture.' Who is the reporter assigned to report on 'the growing danger'? One Neil Puffet.

Colin Orton

What about Jefferson Hack, who is Kate Moss's boyfriend. He's a journalist.

Alice Bedford

While surfing the Net recently, I discovered that the BBC's Hong Kong correspondent is called Damian Grammaticas. For a journalist working for the Beeb, his surname struck me as being tremendously apt.

Maria Mawson

The Sky News reporter at Princess Anne's court appearance was James Forelock (as in tugging one's forelock in deference).

Dennis Snape

How about the Press Association's showbiz correspondent . . . Anita Singh?

Martin Gray

There's a young man on work experience as a writer at the *Daily Mirror*'s 'Sorted' column called Andrew Penman.

Michael Greenwood

ON THE ROAD

When my daughter took her driving test some years ago, the examiner's name was Mr Failer. Despite this unfair distraction, she passed.

S. Wooldridge

A driving instructor in Derby is called Mark Passmore. According to the *Derby Evening Telegraph* (16 October 2002): 'Mark Passmore, 48, has been a driving instructor for 23 years and owns the Passmore School of Motoring. He says his job is not just about mirror, signal, manoeuvre, but more about patience and a sense of humour . . .'

Mr T. J. Drakeley

We have a local driving instructor called Andre Hooton. (Hoot-on, get it? Beep, beep, learner driver.)

Mick Conway

I recently hired some film equipment from a company, Marine Film Services, which rents out and operates boats, diving jobs, commercial charter ships, police boats and all things aquatic. The man who runs it is called Richard Carless.

Claire Otway

While driving down the
Moselle in Germany we
passed a second-hand car
dealer named Heep.

Derek and Anita

Years ago, when I failed my driving test, the
examiner went by the name of Mr Goodenough.

Mr C. McCarron

Our local courier service in Victoria, London, is
run by a man called Andy Wagon – now that is
handy!

Spiros Contomichalos

On a recent news bulletin a French person was
interviewed who had something to do with
France's road transport system, and he was talking
about the effects of snow on French roads. His
name was Jean Delarue, which translates into
'John of the Street'. *Quelle surprise!*

Colin Smale

At the Kwik-Fit tyre and exhaust centre in Brentwood, Essex, works a friendly and helpful manager. His name is Collin Overall.

Shirley Britton

Seen passing through Wigan: Road Haulage by A. Rhodes.

Colin Sayer

The chief executive of the Driving Standards Agency – the body responsible for L-test exams – is called Gary Austin (as in cars).

Clinton Manning

While watching ITV's *Learner Drivers* series, I was amazed to discover that one of the driving instructors was called Michelle Skidmore.

Fiona Byrne

EDUCATION
EDUCATION
EDUCATION

Mrs Elisabeth Eatwell

Food Technology teacher

Tony Achilles

Senior lecturer in podiatry

Kathryn Plant

Biology teacher

My GCSE Food Technology teacher at Amery Hill School, Alton, Hampshire, went by the rather apt name of Mrs (Elisabeth) Eatwell.

Sophie Birks

I have just received the Newcastle University newsletter email from the guy who edits the newsletter: Paul Mailer.

Rob Thorpe

My mum was a school cook for many years and her name is Mary Brusell.

Sally Hastings (née Brusell)

Who is the senior lecturer in podiatry – foot disorders to you and me – at the University of Plymouth? Step forward Tony Achilles.

Name withheld

At my daughter's school, the Head of Religious Studies was called Miss Hosannah.
Alison Boswell

I work at Lancaster University where there is a Dr and Mrs Ion who work in the physics department. My mate wonders if they have a positively charged relationship!
Simon Attwood

My daughter's name is Kathryn Plant. She teaches Biology at Liskeard School, Cornwall.
David Blewett

The special needs teacher at my son's school (North Harringay Infants School), who sets aside time to spend with children who really need it is called Mrs Toogood, which I think is rather nice, because she is.

Claire Otway

The guy who presided over Religious Studies at my cousins' boarding school in St Albans was a Reverend Pine-Coffin.

Anna Day

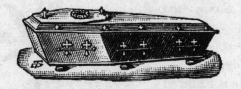

TV
LAND

Sara Blizzard
Weather girl

Sue Kneebone

Make-up artist, Casualty

Sharon Swab
SECOND ASSISTANT
DIRECTOR, *ER*

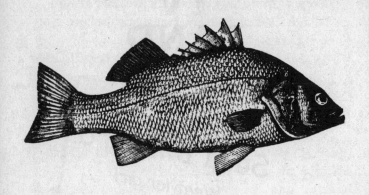

The BBC's weather presenter on Friday opened his forecast with the words 'Nice weather for ducks', before going on to tell us how wet and miserable the next few days will be. Rain, rain and more rain. Who was this presenter? None other than Michael Fish.

Mark Davies

There's a great example on one of the eastern regional news TV teams . . . presenter Debbie Tubby. I bet she's always being asked about being a real-life Telly Tubby.

Paul Fry

There's a young lady who is the weather girl on BBC *East Midlands Today*. Her name, believe it or not, is Sara Blizzard.

Don Burrows, Ian Jardine, Marie Love, Rhisiart Jarman-Harris, L. Hutchinson, John Richardson and Peter Sketchley

How about the weather forecaster on BBC *Look East*? She's called Julie Reinger.

Steve Kelk

The second assistant director on the US hospital drama *ER* is the aptly named Sharon Swab.

Fiona Byrne

The producer of the BBC documentary, *Dunkirk*, which marked the 1940 evacuation from Dunkirk during the Second World War, is called Rob Warr.

Fiona Byrne

The make-up artist on *Casualty* on BBC1 is called Sue Kneebone. The producer of *The Vicar of Dibley* is called Sue Vertue.

John Baker

WATERWORKS

Val Fountain

Anglian Water Press Officer

John Drinkwater

WELL DRILLER

Dr Chris Spray

Northumbrian Water
Environment Director

Some years ago a woman called Val Fountain used to be press officer for Anglian Water.

Pauline Hawkins

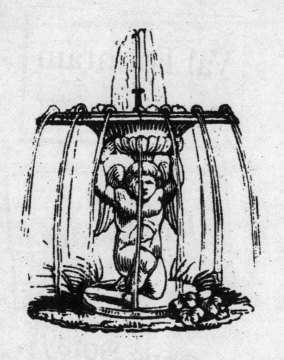

The Environment Director of Northumbrian Water is Dr Chris Spray.

John Heslop

We have a local councillor in Spelthorne who has written to the local paper, the *Herald*, on the subject of flooding. In his letter he talks about the Jubilee River scheme and tells readers how 'water finds its own level' and about 'the Dutch who know about water'. Indeed, the word 'water' is mentioned as many as eight times in his brief letter. And what is the name of this councillor who doubles as an expert on water? Vic . . . Drinkwater.

David Steen

In Rockland, Maine, there was a John Drinkwater – Well Driller.

Gerry

I've just been watching an interview with a senior employee of Thames Water, the London water supplier, on the topic of water-saving tips. His name was Dr Peter Spillett.

Matti Lamphrey

In a public notice printed in the *Daily Mirror* it states that: 'A serious water pollution incident arose at the Lowermoor reservoir, Cornwall, in July 1988. This resulted in contaminated water being supplied to many residences in the Camelford area . . . The Government has set up an independent Expert Group to investigate whether this incident may have had long-term effects upon health . . . If you would like to give evidence contact Mr K. Mistry, Department of Health . . . ' A telling name, indeed.

Dave Harkling

THE FINAL CURTAIN

Frank F. Box

Funeral directors

Wake and Paine

UNDERTAKERS

ALFRED TOMES
AND SONS

MEMORIAL MASONS

A work colleague of mine organized her father's headstone with a firm of memorial masons called Alfred Tomes and Sons, which is based in West London. Her contact is a Mr John Doe. Very apt.

Jason Haddon

When we attended my father-in-law's cremation, the officiating vicar was a Reverend Ash.

Jackie Bowden

Some years ago, while working in the Batley area of West Yorkshire, I laughed every time I drove past Frank F. Box – Funeral Directors.

Alison Rayner

In Cape Town, South Africa, there is a firm of undertakers called Human and Pitt.

Sally Pearce, George Harris and Bob Parrot

An undertaker in Dewsbury is known by the name of Eric Box. All the hearses have 'Box' on their registration plates.

Irene Burton and Patricia Wilby

The priest who conducts funeral services at St Luke's Church, Stone Cross, near Eastbourne, is Father Jonathan Graves.

Steve Purcell

In Hull we have a company of funeral directors who are called Boddy. A case, therefore, of Boddy knowing where the bodies are buried.

T. D. Gray

In Twickenham there is a firm of undertakers called Wake and Paine.

Sally O'Mahony

Enniskillen, County Fermanagh, is home to a firm called Enda Love Funeral Directors. Enda is the bloke who runs it.

Belfaster

IN A LEAGUE OF THEIR OWN – A MISCELLANY

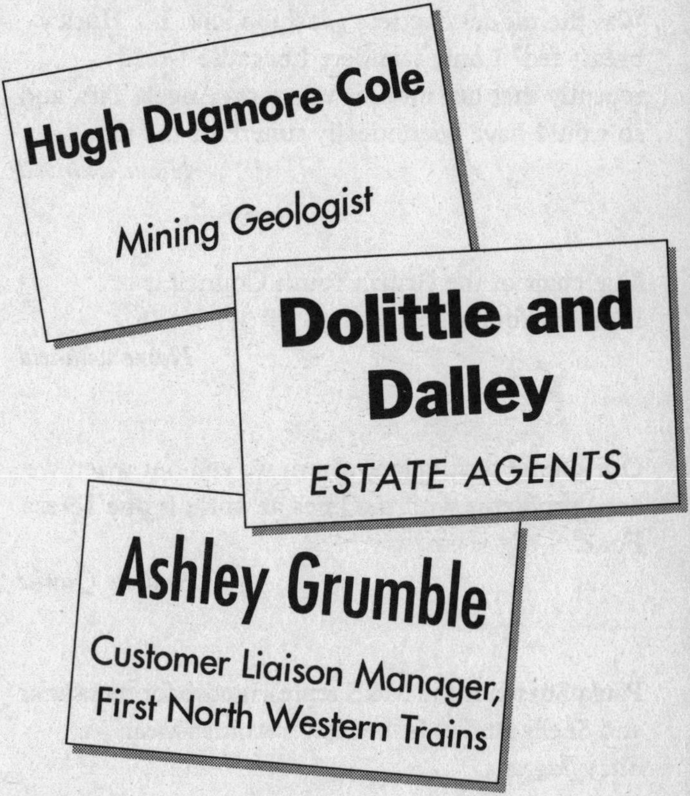

Hugh Dugmore Cole

Mining Geologist

Dolittle and Dalley

ESTATE AGENTS

Ashley Grumble

Customer Liaison Manager,
First North Western Trains

As a young woman I was a hairdresser for fifteen years. My maiden name is Curling.

Joyce Wilkinson

Was the model / actress / fashion icon Liz Hurley breast-fed? I only wondered because I read recently that her mother was born Angela Titt, and so would have been ideally suited for the job.

Name withheld

The chair of the British Youth Council is . . . Blossom Young.

Name withheld

Our phone technician, whom we call out when we have problems with the lines at work, is one Teresa Fone.

Andrew Quirke

Paula Stretch is the M&S representative for menswear and Shelly Ruffles is the rep for womenswear.
Suzy Jagger

A man who works for London's premier purveyor of telescopes is Alex Skye.

Lucy Williams

The man who runs Romeo and Juliets, a sex shop in Stafford, is called Roger Dickin.

Trevor Ball

I was impressed to read about the Met Office forecaster (quoted in the *Guardian*, 12 January 2004) commenting on the gale warnings in force and the tornado / waterspout in the Bristol Channel. His name is Bob Wilderspin.

Wendy Bradley

My son booked his first appointment at a high street opticians and was seen by a Mr Eye.

Norma Miles

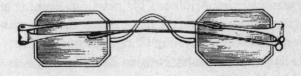

We have an environmental health officer based in Birmingham who covers the Handsworth area of the city. His name is Mr M. Basharat.

Gerry Tickley

In the Basingstoke shop, USA Nails, where they do every conceivable thing to one's toe and fingernails, one of the chaps that works there is a certain Mr Toe.

Richard Chivers

The Stroud District Council Cabinet member for the environment who oversees waste collection and recycling issues is called Councillor Dorcas Binns.

Name withheld

In my Freemasons Lodge in Spain our Almoner is John Legge, hence he is known as Almoner Legge.

Alf Burgess

I was watching Midlands TV news one evening and was surprised to learn from a report that the man responsible for recycling Christmas trees at the Lickey Hills Country Park, in Birmingham, is a Simon Needles.

Phil Smith and Mike Rogers

Our local estate agents are Dolittle and Dalley.

M. Berry

In the late 1960s/early 1970s the chief sanitary inspector for Norwich was a Mr Smellie.

Dave Brusselen

In September 2003 the US military spokesman in Baghdad who was responsible for revealing details to the world's media about a bomb blast in Irbil during the Iraqi war was aptly named Staff Sgt Shane Slaughter.

Nick Sommerlad

The assistant secretary of the Prison Officers' Association is called Duncan Keys.

Claire Otway

When I read a quote given by Station Officer Pugh of York Fire Station on BBC News Online recently, I wondered whether there was any possibility that he could be the same Pugh of 'Hugh, Pugh, Barney McGrew, Cuthbert, Dibble and Grubb' fame, formerly based at Trumpton Fire Station . . . Perhaps he's been promoted?

Dan Douglas

In Widnes market, Cheshire, there is O'Hare's Barber Shop, owned by Mr Patrick O'Hare.

Billy Eaton

Back in the days when broadcast transmitters were made in the US, most of them were made by RCA. The chief engineer of RCA's transmitter division was one R. F. Burns. Those who work on transmitters, radar, microwave ovens, and the like know to be careful to avoid getting radio-frequency burns, more commonly called 'RF burns'.

Gerry

When I was with the fire brigade our commander's name was Firebrace.

Win Harrington

Our two military top dogs in Afghanistan are Colonels Chicken & Curry.

Joe Monro

The estate agents and auctioneers in Newport, Gwent, are Crook and Blight.

Sarah Thurbon

While working for a company in the automotive industry, I had to contact the makers of fire engines to be supplied to the Scottish Fire Service. Their liaison officer was Willy Burns.

Sue Rose

I worked as a prison officer at Pucklechurch Remand Centre near Bristol in the 1970s and 1980s and, at various times during this period, we had the following people employed there . . . The kitchen officer was a Miss Rice; the gardener a Mr Budding; the chaplain went about his daily acts of worship in the name of the Reverend Godden – and, to cap the lot (and reverting to a culinary theme once more), the cook and baker was, initially, a certain Mr Savory. He retired to be replaced by Mr Sage.

Glynis Wright

Jamie House works for estate agents W. J. Meade, based in Bow, East London.

Nick Webster

I gather that a member of staff at Ann Summers changed her name from Cox a few months ago. Now I learn that the boss of Beate Uhse – a German lingerie chain opening up in the UK – is called Gerard Cok!

Clinton Manning

I work in a shop in Earl's Court and our refuse manager who works for Kensington and Chelsea council is called Mr Craig Tidy.

Tom Barnes

Facing Earlestown market was a barber's shop run by a Mr Hackett. According to a friend who called for a haircut, the barber was well named.

L. Corless

We had a public health inspector in this area some years ago, whose name was Cecil Pitt. Of course he was better known as Cesspit.

Tony Richards

Found in my local *Thomson Directory*: 'Curtain alterations, Jenny Hook, Hailsham.'

Nigel Jones

The Liberal Democrat MEP candidate who, in September 2002, wrote a lengthy article in the *Independent* in support of porn law reform, is called Julia Gash; she is a businesswoman who owns a number of erotic boutiques.

Name withheld

In the 1950s I worked at Associated Electrical Industries in Trafford Park, Manchester. The chairman of the board was Mr A. C. Main.

Mr R. W. Hopper

Many years ago, when I was a schoolboy in Coventry, there was an optician with a shop next to the Belgrade Theatre. He was called Hugh Seymour.

Clive Dixon

My friend Alexa, working for the National Youth Theatre this summer, found that the person in charge of wardrobe was James Button.

Carole Luckraft

Have you heard of the portable loo hirers, Owen Pugh (Owe & Poo)?

G. G. Hicks

Published in the *Daily Mirror* in June 2003, there was an item about Monporn Hughes, controller of a multi-million pound prostitution empire of Thai slaves.

Ron Robbin-Coker

The Customer Liaison Manager at First North Western trains in Manchester is Ashley Grumble.

Robin Thornber

Bill Connor (Cassandra in the *Daily Mirror*) on a visit to Plattsburg, New York State, in May 1964, was given access to a US missile bunker. The major in charge – in common with his men – was required to wear a hat with his title inscribed prominently. His name? Major Slaughter.

Brian Saunders

I was watching *Newsnight* yesterday and saw a Unison delegate at Blackpool for the TUC conference. Her name: Sasha Strike!

Tom Rothery

At the bra factory where I worked for many years (Silhouette, in Whitchurch, Shropshire) the boss was a Mr Grabham.

Viv Fletcher

I have a friend who is a mining geologist, working in Carltonville, South Africa, and his name is Hugh Dugmore Cole.

Vicky

A researcher on Channel 4's *More Sex Tips For Girls* was born for her job. She's called Emily Cummings.

Steve Purcell

The BBC have published a book called *Make the Right Move* – a homebuyer's manual designed to guide people safely through the stressful process of buying a property. It's by Nicki Household.

Name withheld

In 1970, while building a large development to Grattan Warehouses head office in Bradford, we employed a consultant drainage engineer called Charles Bott.

Stuart Atkin

The man at Thomson Holidays responsible for assisting customers enquiring about changing their flights is called . . . Harry Helps.

Steve Purcell

The man in charge of the RNLI's door-to-door collections is organizer Andrew Hustler.

Martin Bowring

I learnt today that the president of the Racehorse Owners' Association is a Jim Furlong.

Brian Hamilton Kelly

According to a piece in *The Times* in February 2004, the chairman of the sub-committee that drew up the report on new EU recycling directives (that may result in mass dumping of cars and electrical equipment) is called Paddy Tipping.

C. Collins

I recently saw a poster advertising the services of R. J. Salvage – a company that collects (or salvages) unwanted furniture in Chelmsford.

Fiona Byrne

The Homeless and Housing Needs Manager for Help the Aged is Joe Oldman.

Jon Herman

There's a binman called Brian Binney.

From a newspaper cutting

There is an optician on Moston Lane, Manchester, whose name is Mr D. Igoe.

Alan McNeill

The newly built police station at Sheffield Airport is on Letsby Avenue. A police spokesman confirms: 'The name of the road was suggested by an officer who is no longer in the Force and it went through council planning meetings without anyone realizing it was a joke.'

Tony Pressley

All Michael O'Mara titles are available by post from:

Bookpost, PO Box 29, Douglas, Isle of Man, IM99 1BQ

Credit cards accepted.
Telephone: 01624 677237
Fax: 01624 670923
Email: bookshop@enterprise.net
Internet: www.bookpost.co.uk

Free postage and packing in the UK.

Other Michael O'Mara Humour titles:

All Men Are Bastards – ISBN 1-85479-387-X pb £3.99
The Book of Urban Legends – ISBN 1-85479-932-0 pb £3.99
The Complete Book of Farting – ISBN 1-85479-440-X pb £4.99
Complete Crap – ISBN 1-85479-313-6 pb £3.99
The Ultimate Book of Farting – ISBN 1-85479-596-1 hb £5.99
The Ultimate Insult – ISBN 1-85479-288-1 pb £5.99
Wicked Cockney Rhyming Slang – ISBN 1-85479-386-1 pb £3.99
Wicked Geordie English – ISBN 1-85479-342-X pb £3.99
Wicked Scouse English – ISBN 1-84317-006-X pb £3.99
The Wicked Wit of Jane Austen – ISBN 1-85479-652-6 hb £9.99
The Wicked Wit of Winston Churchill – ISBN 1-85479-529-5 hb £9.99
The Wicked Wit of Oscar Wilde – ISBN 1-85479-542-2 hb £9.99
The World's Stupidest Criminals – ISBN 1-85479-879-0 pb £3.99
The World's Stupidest Graffiti – ISBN 1-85479-876-6 pb £3.99
The World's Stupidest Laws – ISBN 1-85479-549-X pb £3.99
The World's Stupidest Men – ISBN 1-85479-508-2 pb £3.99
The World's Stupidest Signs – ISBN 1-85479-555-4 pb £3.99
More of the World's Stupidest Signs – ISBN 1-84317-032-9 pb £4.99
The World's Stupidest Last Words – ISBN 1-84317-021-3 pb £4.99
The World's Stupidest Inventions – ISBN 1-84317-036-1 pb £5.99
The World's Stupidest Instructions – ISBN 1-84317-078-7 pb £4.99
The World's Stupidest Sporting Screw-Ups – ISBN 1-84317-039-6 pb £4.99
Shite's Unoriginal Miscellany – ISBN 1-84317-064-7 hb £9.99
Cricket: It's A Funny Old Game – ISBN 1-84317-090-6 pb £4.99
Football: It's A Funny Old Game – ISBN 1-84317-091-4 pb £4.99